The Temptations of Jesus Christ

Book 8

by Daniel Strasel

THE 3f STUDY OF CHRISTIANITY

Copyright © August 5, 2024 by Daniel W. Strasel

All rights reserved.

First printed in the United States of America.

Synopsis:

This book discusses in detail Matthew Chapter 4 verses 1-11.

Http://www.Mirroranium.com

ISBN: 978-1-947052-08-6

faith   fealty   forgiveness

The Temptations of Jesus Christ

Table of Contents

Page 4	Opening the Study
Page 5	The Author of Matthew
Page 6	Matthew Chapter 4:1-11
Page 7	Examining Matthew 4
Page 10	The First Temptation
Page 13	The Second Temptation
Page 18	The Third Temptation
Page 23	Ending Session Wrap-up
Page 24	Closing Prayer
Page 25	About the Author

by Daniel Strasel

THE 3f STUDY OF CHRISTIANITY

Opening the Study

"Our Lord Jesus Christ, please help us to receive Your Word with open minds and hearts, judging only with righteous judgment. Please help us to be wise and alert so that we are not misled. Please bless this study, Lord. Please help us to be filled with and to exude the fruits of the Spirit, which are: Peace, Love, Joy, Patience, Goodness, Kindness, Faithfulness, Gentility, Humility, and perhaps above all, Self-Control. Please help us to be good servants, good friends, and good neighbors: encouraging and receiving one another in and with love. Please be with us in this study of Your temptations, that we might better understand our own temptations, and be convicted and saved in our acknowledgment of our failures. That we might better endure as temptation comes upon us. Thank You, Lord, for Your mercy and Your grace. Thank You for Your Word. Thank You for Your love. In the name of the Lord Jesus Christ, Yeshua, Yehoshua, son of God, Amen."

The temptations of Christ are recorded in the book of Matthew, and then again in the book of Luke.

First we'll read Matthew Chapter 4 verses 1-11 completely through, then we'll look at them each in detail.

faith　　　　　　　　　fealty　　　　　　　　　forgiveness

The Author of Matthew

Yet, before we start reading, we should ask: who is the author? Who *is* Matthew? And though we might spend a great deal of time talking about who he was as a person, what we need to establish for *this* session is that Matthew is one of the twelve disciples chosen by Jesus Christ. This account then comes from a firsthand witness and companion of the Lord.

Now, if you investigate, you will find that some would argue that the author of the book is anonymous. Though, not long after Matthew died, Papias of Hierapolis – who lived from 60-130 A.D. – gives credit to Matthew as the author, which then would have been the common understanding at the time as the Gospel of Matthew was extremely popular and widely distributed. There are many respected 1st and 2nd century historians and theologians who have also given credit unto Matthew, as well as innumerous others over the last 2 thousand years.

The argument against his authorship then is comparatively recent, and therefore *most* speculative as it is furthest from the source. In the end, of course, it's a matter of where you put your faith – but, as we discussed in Session 1 of our study: *almost everything is a matter of faith*, and where you put it.

by Daniel Strasel

THE 3f STUDY OF CHRISTIANITY

Matthew 4

1 Then was Jesus led up of the Spirit into the wilderness to be tempted of the devil.
2 And when he had fasted forty days and forty nights, he was afterward an hungred.
3 And when the tempter came to him, he said, If thou be the Son of God, command that these stones be made bread.
4 But he answered and said, It is written, Man shall not live by bread alone, but by every word that proceedeth out of the mouth of God.
5 Then the devil taketh him up into the holy city, and setteth him on a pinnacle of the temple,
6 And saith unto him, If thou be the Son of God, cast thyself down: for it is written, He shall give his angels charge concerning thee: and in their hands they shall bear thee up, lest at any time thou dash thy foot against a stone.
7 Jesus said unto him, It is written again, Thou shalt not tempt the Lord thy God.
8 Again, the devil taketh him up into an exceeding high mountain, and sheweth him all the kingdoms of the world, and the glory of them;
9 And saith unto him, All these things will I give thee, if thou wilt fall down and worship me.
10 Then saith Jesus unto him, Get thee hence, Satan: for it is written, Thou shalt worship the Lord thy God, and him only shalt thou serve.
11 Then the devil leaveth him, and, behold, angels came and ministered unto him.

faith fealty forgiveness

The Temptations of Jesus Christ

Examining Matthew 4

1 Then was Jesus led up of the Spirit into the wilderness to be tempted of the devil.

Then was Jesus

When? Right after He was baptized by John the Baptist. Let's quickly read what's happened right before He is led in Chapter 3 verses 13 through 17.

Matthew Chapter 3

> 13 Then cometh Jesus from Galilee to Jordan unto John, to be baptized of him.
> 14 But John forbad him, saying, I have need to be baptized of thee, and comest thou to me?
> 15 And Jesus answering said unto him, Suffer it to be so now: for thus it becometh us to fulfil all righteousness. Then he suffered him.
> 16 And Jesus, when he was baptized, went up straightway out of the water: and, lo, the heavens were opened unto him, and he saw the Spirit of God descending like a dove, and lighting upon him:
> 17 And lo a voice from heaven, saying, This is my beloved Son, in whom I am well pleased.

Led up of the ***Spirit***

Who is leading? The Spirit. In the Greek, it's "pneuma," meaning breath, spirit, soul. It is used 385 times in the NT, most often rendered as "Holy Ghost" or "Spirit of God".

Here also we have a complete manifestation of the trinity: The voice of the Father, the personage of the Son, and the presence of the Spirit.

by Daniel Strasel

Into the *wilderness*

Why the wilderness? This is a contrast to when Israel was wandering in the wilderness after crossing the Red Sea, escaping the captivity of Egypt. We'll find the reason in Deuteronomy Chapter 8 verse 2.

Deuteronomy 8

> 2 And thou shalt remember all the way which the LORD thy God led thee these forty years in the wilderness, to humble thee, and to prove thee, to know what was in thine heart, whether thou wouldest keep his commandments, or no.

To be *tempted*

Tempted? So, what is a **temptation**? Ice cream? Only if you're hungry. In other words, a temptation is something you want. Though further, the temptation is to prove thee and see if thou wouldst keep his commandments or no. Whether thou wouldst keep His commandments or no? The **temptation** is to *sin*.

What could possibly be a temptation of the Lord…to *sin*? We shall see. Something the Lord wants, that the act of acting upon would violate His own law.

Of the *Devil*.

Who? He who tempts every man to sin. We cover the enemy in detail in Session 5.

2 And when he had fasted forty days and forty nights, he was afterward an hungred.

And when he had fasted *forty days and forty nights*

faith   fealty   forgiveness

The Temptations of Jesus Christ

Why 40 days and 40 nights? The Lord is mirroring Moses receiving the Law. Let's take a quick look at Exodus Chapter 34, verses 27 & 28.

Exodus 34

> 27 And the LORD said unto Moses, Write thou these words: for after the tenor of these words I have made a covenant with thee and with Israel.
> 28 And he was there with the LORD forty days and forty nights; he did neither eat bread, nor drink water. And he wrote upon the tables the words of the covenant, the ten commandments.

"For after the tenor of these words" is a bit tricky. "Tenor" in Hebrew is "peh" (Pey Yod), which means "from the mouth." The Pey is also a letter in Hebrew that means mouth. The Interlinear translation reads "for on the mouth of these words I will cut a covenant" *For after the tenor of these words* might perhaps better be understood if expressed as "for by my mouth with these words do I make a covenant with thee."

When Christ thrice thwarts the tempter, he does it by quoting the Law (The Torah - authored by Moses) all three times. He also then illustrates that He obeys the Law - the Law that He wrote.

He was afterward an ***hungred***.

Hungered. Well of course He's hungered - He hasn't eaten for 40 days! "Hungered" in the Greek is 'peinao,' meaning famished, but then also same as 'penace,' meaning 'starving.'

Christ is
literally
now
starving
to death.

by Daniel Strasel

THE 3f STUDY OF CHRISTIANITY

THE FIRST TEMPTATION

3 And when the tempter came to him, he said, If thou be the Son of God, command that these stones be made bread.

And when the *tempter*

Here he is called "the tempter" by Matthew using the Greek word 'peirazo.' The next 2 times he will be called 'the devil', or 'diabolos' in Greek.

This time he doesn't display power, and simply seems to appeal to reason...perhaps even in an almost nonchalant fashion. He might even shrug as he says something to the tune of: "Why are you starving to death? If/Since you're the Son of God, why not make just these stones into bread and eat and save your life?"

Remember his conversation with Eve in Genesis 3:1-5:

Genesis 3

1 Now the serpent was more subtil than any beast of the field which the LORD God had made. And he said unto the woman, Yea, hath God said, Ye shall not eat of every tree of the garden?
2 And the woman said unto the serpent, We may eat of the fruit of the trees of the garden:
3 But of the fruit of the tree which is in the midst of the garden, God hath said, Ye shall not eat of it, neither shall ye touch it, lest ye die.
4 And the serpent said unto the woman, Ye shall not surely die:
5 For God doth know that in the day ye eat thereof, then your eyes shall be opened, and ye shall be as gods, knowing good and evil.

What is the temptation?
What is the sin?

faith　　　　　　　fealty　　　　　　　forgiveness

The Temptations of Jesus Christ

Well, He's literally starving to death. He's hungry, He's weak. He's been completely alone for over a month, enduring, I imagine, 40 *very* long days and nights.

The temptation is to use His authority to turn stones to bread to give Him the sustenance to save His life.

The *sin* would be not trusting in God to provide for Him as God sees fit - that perhaps God somehow forgot about Him, or wasn't (isn't) present and is unaware of His Son's peril. The sin is that He knows the path set before Him (He knows He is there to be tempted), yet then He personally changes the course.

<u>4 But he answered and said, It is written, Man shall not live by bread alone, but by every word that proceedeth out of the mouth of God.</u>

The Lord is quoting directly from Deuteronomy, Chapter 8 verse 3.

Deuteronomy 8

> 3 And he humbled thee, and suffered thee to hunger, and fed thee with manna, which thou knewest not, neither did thy fathers know; that he might make thee know that man doth not live by bread only, but by every word that proceedeth out of the mouth of the LORD doth man live.

This passage was addressed to the wandering nation of Israel; about how they were given manna when they needed it, for exactly how long they needed it for – further demonstrated that it (the manna) only ever lasted a *single* day, ***except*** for the manna that fell the day before the Sabbath, for *that* manna instead lasted 2 days. God was present, aware of them and their need, and provided for them.

It is by the Lord's will alone – not by bread nor by luck – that we are alive. If we are to have the bread to sustain us, the Lord will provide it. If you need bread, ask.

by Daniel Strasel

THE 3f STUDY OF CHRISTIANITY

Matthew 7

> 7 Ask, and it shall be given you; seek, and ye shall find; knock, and it shall be opened unto you:
> 8 For every one that asketh receiveth; and he that seeketh findeth; and to him that knocketh it shall be opened.
> 9 Or what man is there of you, whom if his son ask bread, will he give him a stone?
> 10 Or if he ask a fish, will he give him a serpent?
> 11 If ye then, being evil, know how to give good gifts unto your children, how much more shall your Father which is in heaven give good things to them that ask him?
> 12 Therefore all things whatsoever ye would that men should do to you, do ye even so to them: for this is the law and the prophets.

John 6

> 32 Then Jesus said unto them, Verily, verily, I say unto you, Moses gave you not that bread from heaven; but my Father giveth you the true bread from heaven.
> 33 For the bread of God is he which cometh down from heaven, and giveth life unto the world.
> 34 Then said they unto him, Lord, evermore give us this bread.
> 35 And Jesus said unto them, I am the bread of life: he that cometh to me shall never hunger; and he that believeth on me shall never thirst.
> 36 But I said unto you, That ye also have seen me, and believe not.
> 37 All that the Father giveth me shall come to me; and him that cometh to me I will in no wise cast out.
> 38 For I came down from heaven, not to do mine own will, but the will of him that sent me.
> 39 And this is the Father's will which hath sent me, that of all which he hath given me I should lose nothing, but should raise it up again at the last day.
> 40 And this is the will of him that sent me, that every one which seeth the Son, and believeth on him, may have everlasting life: and I will raise him up at the last day.

faith   fealty   forgiveness

THE SECOND TEMPTATION

<u>5 Then the devil taketh him up into the holy city, and setteth him on a pinnacle of the temple,</u>

Then the ***devil*** taketh him up into the ***holy city***,

Now he's the *devil*, the 'diabolos', and he's showing off his power – possibly trying to frighten the Lord, if possible.

The Holy city is Jerusalem, where the temple is located. (Zerubbabel's & Ezra's Temple, then refurbished and expanded by Herod in 20 B.C. - not Solomon's).

and setteth him on a ***pinnacle*** of the temple.

A pinnacle is one of the tallest points – at this time about 450 feet up. Christ is likely holding on for dear life.

<u>6 And saith unto him, If thou be the Son of God, cast thyself down: for it is written, He shall give his angels charge concerning thee: and in their hands they shall bear thee up, lest at any time thou dash thy foot against a stone.</u>

Now the devil is scoffing at the Word of God: "*It is written,*" he says, throwing it back at Christ. He's additionally presenting several subtextual challenges: "Or don't you *trust* God? Or maybe you're *not* the Son? Maybe there is no God – no God here greater than I."

What is the temptation?
What is the <u>sin</u>?

Christ is tired. Exhausted. Starving. Weak. Bullied. Alone.

by Daniel Strasel

The temptation is to jump and rely on the Father to save Him from His position.

The <u>sin</u> would be in testing God – to insist He demonstrate or perform in order to prove His love and presence.

The devil is *misquoting* Psalm 91, verses 11 & 12.

Psalm 91

> 11 For he shall give his angels charge over thee, to keep thee in all thy ways.
> 12 They shall bear thee up in their hands, lest thou dash thy foot against a stone.

"To keep thee in all thy ways." What a curious line to omit.

"Keep" in Hebrew is "Shamar," meaning 'guard,' 'protect,' 'hedge.' "Ways" in Hebrew is "Derek," meaning 'road,' 'journey,' 'course'.

Imagine being in a hedge maze, and at every intersection you are offered many choices as to which direction you might take. At each intersection the ends are all unknown - except for one - for one is always marked to take you to God.

Our decisions matter. If we willingly pursue self-destruction – if we willingly turn away from God – God may send his angels to keep us in all our ways. God **will** send His angels to keep us if we seek His way.

Homework: read all of Psalm 91.

As we learned in Section 5, the enemy has to ask for permission to accost you. God *put* Christ on that path. God permitted the enemy to put Him on the pinnacle.
If the devil threw Him down without permission, His angels would

The Temptations of Jesus Christ

have absolutely, instantly been there.

The problem *here* is that by jumping, it would be His own decision rather than to put His faith in God; that God would keep Him & *was* keeping Him. In Daniel Chapter 3, Shadrach, Meshach, and Abednego didn't *jump* into the furnace, they were cast into it. In Daniel Chapter 6, Daniel didn't camp out in the lion's den, he was cast into there.

If they **chose** to do those things, it would be an attempt to brag about their great faith, and then require God perform for them to deliver them from their folly.

Also, as He is at the Holy temple, jumping down from the pinnacle would be quite a spectacle to the many inhabitants and visitors – but it wasn't His time to announce Himself - it wasn't His way.

7 Jesus said unto him, It is written again, Thou shalt not tempt the Lord thy God.

It is written AGAIN? But, the Lord's first rebuke was about bread and the word of God; He didn't say anything about tempting God.
Yet, the first tempting of the Lord is present when you understand that the appearance of manna in the wilderness came **after** Israel first provoked God. First, let's look at Exodus 16:2-8 to see the first temptation of God by the people of Israel as they wandered in the wilderness.

Exodus 16

> 2 And the whole congregation of the children of Israel murmured against Moses and Aaron in the wilderness:
> 3 And the children of Israel said unto them, Would to God we had died by the hand of the LORD in the land of Egypt, when we sat by the flesh pots, and when we did eat bread to the full; for ye have brought us forth into this wilderness, to kill this whole assembly with hunger.

by Daniel Strasel

THE 3f STUDY OF CHRISTIANITY

Exodus 16

> 4 Then said the LORD unto Moses, Behold, I will rain bread from heaven for you; and the people shall go out and gather a certain rate every day, that I may prove them, whether they will walk in my law, or no.
> 5 And it shall come to pass, that on the sixth day they shall prepare that which they bring in; and it shall be twice as much as they gather daily.
> 6 And Moses and Aaron said unto all the children of Israel, At even, then ye shall know that the LORD hath brought you out from the land of Egypt:
> 7 And in the morning, then ye shall see the glory of the LORD; for that he heareth your murmurings against the LORD: and what are we, that ye murmur against us?
> 8 And Moses said, This shall be, when the LORD shall give you in the evening flesh to eat, and in the morning bread to the full; for that the LORD heareth your murmurings which ye murmur against him: and what are we? your murmurings are not against us, but against the LORD.

Your murmurings are not against us, but **against the Lord**.

In saying "It is written *again*," Christ is now referencing the **second** time Israel tempted God. He is quoting Deuteronomy 6:16.

Deuteronomy 6

> 16 Ye shall not tempt the LORD your God, as ye tempted him in Massah.

And to understand the incident at Massah, we need to read Exodus 17:1-7.

Exodus 17

> 1 And all the congregation of the children of Israel journeyed from the wilderness of Sin, after their journeys, according to the com-

faith   fealty   forgiveness

The Temptations of Jesus Christ

Exodus 17

> mandment of the LORD, and pitched in Rephidim: and there was no water for the people to drink.
> 2 Wherefore the people did chide with Moses, and said, Give us water that we may drink. And Moses said unto them, Why chide ye with me? wherefore do ye tempt the LORD?
> 3 And the people thirsted there for water; and the people murmured against Moses, and said, Wherefore is this that thou hast brought us up out of Egypt, to kill us and our children and our cattle with thirst?
> 4 And Moses cried unto the LORD, saying, What shall I do unto this people? they be almost ready to stone me.
> 5 And the LORD said unto Moses, Go on before the people, and take with thee of the elders of Israel; and thy rod, wherewith thou smotest the river, take in thine hand, and go.
> 6 Behold, I will stand before thee there upon the rock in Horeb; and thou shalt smite the rock, and there shall come water out of it, that the people may drink. And Moses did so in the sight of the elders of Israel.
> 7 And he called the name of the place Massah, and Meribah, because of the chiding of the children of Israel, and because they tempted the LORD, saying, Is the LORD among us, or not?

"Chide" in Hebrew is "reeb," which means to toss, grapple, complain, rebuke.

"Murmur" in the Hebrew is "loon" or "leen," and means to complain, to be obstinate, to hold onto a grudge.

The tempting is: "*Is* God *really* here? Does He *really* love us?" He is. He does. Do not test the love of God. Do not complain if the bread is not before you at *your time*. Your hunger is your test.

Christ is telling the devil He will not tempt the love of God; He will not <u>test</u> the <u>promise</u> of God. He has faith in it without demonstration. Thou shalt not tempt the Lord thy God. He is also telling the devil directly: Do not tempt <u>**Me**</u>.

by Daniel Strasel

THE 3f STUDY OF CHRISTIANITY

THE THIRD TEMPTATION

<u>8 Again, the devil taketh him up into an exceeding high mountain, and sheweth him all the kingdoms of the world, and the glory of them;
9 And saith unto him, All these things will I give thee, if thou wilt fall down and worship me.</u>

The devil claims he owns and controls all the kingdoms of the world, and that he has the ability to give them to Christ. Christ does not challenge that claim - He will later even personally affirm it.

John 12

> 31 Now is the judgment of this world: now shall the prince of this world be cast out.

"Prince" in Greek is "archon, meaning first, chief, prince, ruler.

John 14

> 30 Hereafter I will not talk much with you: for the prince of this world cometh, and hath nothing in me.

Archon, again.

John 16

> 11 Of judgment, because the prince of this world is judged.

Archon, again.

The ruler of this world.

Gone is the scoffing of the devil. He has completely dropped the "If thou be the Son of God" rhetoric. *Now* the devil goes directly to the point, as if saying: "Tell you what, I'll make a deal with you: you worship me, and I'll have all the people of the Earth worship you.

faith   fealty   forgiveness

The Temptations of Jesus Christ

"***You need not die*** for their sins, for they will no longer be led into sinning. You will have all the wealth and love of the world - always from now on. No more tragedy. No more sickness, no more suffering. I will stop accusing and tempt no more. I will no longer confuse the truth or lay snares."

What is the temptation?
What is the <u>sin</u>?

The temptation is that Christ can avoid going to the cross if He worship Satan before God. We will see in a moment the extent to which Christ wished to avoid the cross; He prayed to God ***3 times*** to be spared that fate.

<u>***The sin***</u> would be to worship anything other than God. To worship the saving of His own life above the Will of God.

Matthew 26

> 39 And he went a little farther, and fell on his face, and prayed, saying, O my Father, if it be possible, let this cup pass from me: nevertheless not as I will, but as thou wilt.

"If it be possible…nevertheless…as **Thou** wilt."

If there were *any other way* to redeem mankind, Christ's prayers were not answered.

Matthew 26

> 41 Watch and pray, that ye enter not into temptation: the spirit indeed is willing, but the flesh is weak.

The flesh is weak. He admits His struggle.

by Daniel Strasel

THE 3f STUDY OF CHRISTIANITY

Matthew 26

> 42 He went away again the second time, and prayed, saying, O my Father, if this cup may not pass away from me, except I drink it, thy will be done.

As if to say: "**Please** don't require this of Me! Yet, I trust You, Your judgments, and Your demands. I defer to Your will."

Matthew 26

> 44 And he left them, and went away again, and prayed the third time, saying the same words.

Luke 22

> 44 And being in an agony he prayed more earnestly: and his sweat was as it were great drops of blood falling down to the ground.

Being in agony He prayed more earnestly. Every time He prayed, He prayed more emphatically – yet always ended with **complete submission** to the Will of God.

This is a model as to how we should pray.

10 Then saith Jesus unto him, Get thee hence, Satan: for it is written, Thou shalt worship the Lord thy God, and him only shalt thou serve.

This offer couldn't be any more insulting: the created tells its creator to worship it.

Then saith Jesus unto him, Get thee hence, Satan

Only the Lord can command the devil; this time I imagine in complete disgust.

For it is written, Thou shalt worship the Lord thy God, and him only

faith   fealty   forgiveness

The Temptations of Jesus Christ

shalt thou serve.

Christ is referencing Deuteronomy 6:4-5, Exodus 20:3, and Exodus 34:14.

Deuteronomy 6 (the Shema: the great commandment)

4 Hear, O Israel: The LORD our God is one LORD: 5 And thou shalt love the LORD thy God with all thine heart, and with all thy soul, and with all thy might.

He is **one** Lord.   Love God with all of what you are, and as much as you can.

Exodus 20

3 Thou shalt have no other gods before me.

No other.

Exodus 34

14 For thou shalt worship no other god

No other.

11 Then the devil leaveth him, and, behold, angels came and ministered unto him.

The devil brought Him to that place and stranded Him there when he departed; He didn't strand Himself there…and behold!

The Father was *always* aware, **He was always there**; He (Jesus) was never far from care.

And neither are we.   Confidently - though devoid of pride - put your whole faith in God.

by Daniel Strasel

Job 13

> 15 Though he slay me, yet will I trust in him: but I will maintain mine own ways before him.

"Though He *slay* me, <u>*yet*</u> will I **trust** in Him."

Psalms 62

> 5 My soul, wait thou only upon God; for my expectation is from him.
> 6 He only is my rock and my salvation: he is my defence; I shall not be moved.
> 7 In God is my salvation and my glory: the rock of my strength, and my refuge, is in God.
> 8 Trust in him at all times; ye people, pour out your heart before him: God is a refuge for us. Selah

Proverbs 3

> 5 Trust in the LORD with all thine heart; and lean not unto thine own understanding.
> 6 In all thy ways acknowledge him, and he shall direct thy paths

You cannot control your life, but you do choose your path.

Our decisions matter.

faith   fealty   forgiveness

The Temptations of Jesus Christ

End of session wrap-up

How & Why does Luke's account differ?

How: Luke omits certain portions of quoted Scripture, and then also changes the order of the temptations by placing the mountain/kingdoms offer 2nd and the pinnacle of the temple 3rd.

Why: Why? My answer is speculative: Unlike Matthew, Luke was not a firsthand witness. I can only suppose that he made the order as such to illustrate that the angels of God were available to Christ ***immediately upon His refusal*** to tempt God to see if they were available in the first place.

Open up to Questions, discussion.

Don't forget your homework! Read all of Psalm 91.

You might also then read Acts 17:11, which might suggest to you that you should read more.

by Daniel Strasel

Closing prayer:

"Thank You, our Lord Jesus Christ! Thank You for bringing us, one and all, to this study of your trials and temptations. Please help us to learn something of ourselves and those around us. Please help us to learn how to fear You and how to love You appropriately. Please help us to understand Your will for all of us, and for each of us, that we might celebrate together Your success for all eternity. Thank You, Lord, for our lives. Thank You for our community. Thank You for our many gifts and many blessings! Please guide us, Lord. Please guide our leaders – whom You have established. Please help us to be good servants and stewards of Your Word. Help us to put our whole faith and trust in You. In the name of Jesus Christ: Yeshua the Messiah, the Mosiach Nagid, Moshiach ben Yoself, God of Adam, of Noah, of Abraham, of Isaac, of Jacob, of David, of Israel, of the Torah, the Tenach, the Bible. Creator of the heavens and the Earth, and all within. Yod Hey Vav Hey, Elohim, the Aleph and the Tav, Adonnai, El, El-Shaddai, Yah. Thank You, shepherd. Thank You, our king. Thank You, our friend! Thank You for your impossible love! Please help us to love as You love, forgive as You forgive, to trust as You trust. Please help our faith, Lord. Please help us to take rest and refuge in You, Your Word, Your promise. Praise be to God; Hallelujah! Amen."

faith   fealty   forgiveness

About the Author

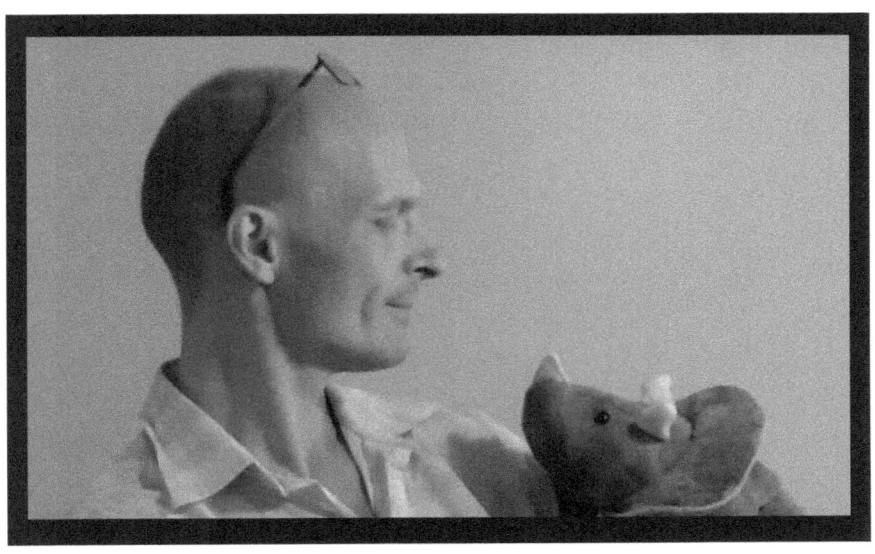

"We are all special - just not for the reasons that we think we are."

Daniel Strasel, born September 15, 1973, Author, Artist, Painter, Philosopher, Theologian, Photographer, Publisher, Developer, Composer, Server, & Friend.

A *shadow* (Psalm 144:4 Man is like to vanity: his days are as a shadow that passeth away. Psalm 102:11 My days are like a shadow that declineth; and I am withered like grass. Job 8:9 For we are but of yesterday, and know nothing, because our days upon earth are a shadow).

A *vapor* (James 4:14 Whereas ye know not what shall be on the morrow. For what is your life? It is even a vapour, that appeareth for a little time, and then vanisheth away).

A *blade of grass* (Isaiah 40:6 All flesh is grass, and all the goodliness thereof is as the flower of the field. 1 Peter 1:24 For all flesh is as grass, and all the glory of man as the flower of grass. The grass withereth, and the flower thereof falleth away:).

Psalm 90:12 So teach us to number our days, that we may apply our hearts unto wisdom.

by Daniel Strasel